Original title:
The Mango Tree's Shadow

Copyright © 2025 Creative Arts Management OÜ
All rights reserved.

Author: Ophelia Ravenscroft
ISBN HARDBACK: 978-1-80586-462-2
ISBN PAPERBACK: 978-1-80586-934-4

Secrets in the Sunlight

Underneath the leafy cheer,
Squirrels giggle, never fear.
A crow drops seeds with great delight,
While ants march on, a funny sight.

The sunlight winks, the breeze jokes loud,
As bugs dance proudly, feeling proud.
We hide behind a laughing glance,
Nature's stage, a joyful dance.

Shadows of Rejuvenation

Lazily sprawled, the cat does snooze,
On cool, dark ground, with nothing to lose.
The sun's bright rays, a comedy show,
While insects juggle, putting on a glow.

A butterfly slips, flaps like a clown,
Buzzing bees in a hustle and frown.
The world's a stage for this laughing spree,
Nature's jesters, just wait and see!

Nature's Gentle Veil

Leaves whisper secrets in laughter's tone,
Twigs play tag, a frolic all their own.
A breeze tickles pretending to chase,
While sunlight plays peek-a-boo with grace.

The groundhog slips, a comic release,
As rabbits bounce in their playful lease.
Nature's playground, a circus of fun,
Where joy is born in the warmth of the sun.

Guardian of Solitude

In solitude's embrace, the shadows grin,
A lizard lounges, wearing a skin.
The world outside is a noisy affair,
But here, the silence hums with flair.

A gopher pops up, a curious trick,
Only to vanish, oh so quick!
Under this shade, the laughter flows,
In a quiet spot, where fun still grows.

Beneath the Canopy of Greeted Light

Under the spread of leaves so wide,
Laughter and giggles playfully collide.
A squirrel in shades, sporting a cap,
Snatching my lunch in a great little flap.

The sunlight dances, playful and bright,
As picnic ants march in a funny fight.
Jokes written in shadows, a comic fame,
Who knew a tree could have such a name?

Whispers of Sun-Kissed Leaves

Breezes tickle, leaves start to chatter,
As bees polish their shoes with some sweet batter.
I sip on sweet tea, it's a sticky affair,
My hat flies away, but I do not care.

A laugh from a crow wearing tiny shoes,
He caws out a riddle, I'm left with the blues.
Oh, nature's jokes are not hard to read,
I'm just here for snacks, not to take heed!

Beneath the Swaying Boughs

Under branches that twist and weave,
Nature's own stage, I hardly believe.
A goat on a branch, what a sight to behold,
In a tutu of leaves, he's pleasantly bold.

The shadows play tricks as I toss them a grin,
A band of ducks waddle, hoping to win.
In this quirky arena, we laugh without strife,
Who knew that a tree could host such a life?

Dance of the Golden Fruit

Swinging fruit drop like jokes on a cue,
Each one's a laughter waiting for you.
A monkey throws one, it bounces just right,
I dodge it with flair, what a fantastic fright!

A picnic goes wild with a fit of delight,
As dance-offs commence under sun's warm sight.
Fruits laughing back, can't keep up with pace,
In this humor-filled garden, I've found my place!

Guardians of the Afternoon

Beneath the leafy giants, a troupe convenes,
Squirrels plot mischief, like furry machines.
With acorns for swords, they dance and they play,
While birds toss in jokes, brightening the day.

A chubby old dog, with a belly so round,
Claims the cool patch and spreads on the ground.
His snores rise like music, a soft, funny tune,
As butterflies giggle and swoop 'neath the moon.

Nestled in Nature's Arms

A gopher peeks out, wearing shades that he found,
He sneezes, and giggles, then tumbles around.
While ants march in lines, with crumbs on parade,
They form a conga, making mischief displayed.

The sunlight filters through, weaving jokes in the air,
Casting goofy patterns that dance everywhere.
A rabbit with glasses reads jokes off a leaf,
While nature applauds with a rustle beneath.

The Poetry of Shade

In the cloak of coolness, a cat takes her nap,
Dreaming of tuna and a sunbeam mishap.
A crow caws a pun, as she shifts in her dream,
Creating a scene, like a sitcom's gleam.

Three frogs in a row, with their silly high leaps,
Compete for the title of craziest creeps.
They ribbit in laughter, rounding off their show,
While sunlight spills down, putting on a glow.

Laughter on a Gentle Breeze

A playful old tortoise with a grin like a pie,
Challenges a hare to a slowpoke sky-high.
With each hesitant step, the crowd gathers near,
Cheering for patience, and munching on cheer.

The breeze carries giggles, from the blooms all around,
As flowers converse in whimsical sound.
A ladybug twirls, on a leaf's dizzy edge,
Leaving a trail of chuckles, like a colorful pledge.

A Refuge of Silence

In the yard, I sneak away,
To the spot where cats like to play.
Birds gossip, squirrels do prance,
I watch them all with a sideways glance.

A crumpled napkin, a snack for me,
No one knows, it's our secret spree.
Breezes rustle like whispering friends,
Until that loud ice cream truck ends.

I pretend to nap, with honeyed sighs,
As ants march home beneath bright skies.
Who knew a spot could hold such cheer,
If only the neighbors would disappear!

Colors of Sunlight

The sun spills laughter on the ground,
Where colors dance and twirl around.
A bluejay laughing at my old hat,
Winds catch my shirt, like a clown in chat.

I scatter crumbs for passersby,
While a toddler laughs as the pigeons fly.
The flowers giggle in a chorus out loud,
Even the dandelions wear a proud shroud.

Oh, how the rays can tickle your nose,
As butterflies waltz near sneaky toes.
The day is bright, with joy in each beam,
Nature's funny, it's one sweet dream!

Sunkissed Serenity

Sunshine bakes my garden's pie,
As I sip lemonade, oh me, oh my!
A lizard does a shuffle, oh what a show,
And my hat flies off, too light to tow.

The grass invites a backyard race,
But I trip over my shoelace in haste.
Giggles erupt from the hedges near,
Did that rabbit just wink, or am I sheer?

A picnic fork seems lost in the fray,
As ants parade in a fine buffet.
Sunkissed laughter fills the air,
With a touch of chaos, oh how rare!

Whispers in the Wind

The breeze tickles my ears with tales,
Of lazy days and tiny snails.
Each gust feels like my old friend's tease,
Makes me chuckle beneath the trees.

Clouds float by like thoughts on a stroll,
I squint and wonder which shape's my goal.
A lazy bear, or a silly old shoe?
Imagination runs wild, as it will do.

A kite swoops low, seeking a duel,
While I perch like a bird, feeling quite cool.
It's a day for giggles, perhaps a prank,
Nature's humor is such a delightful flank!

Laughter Echoing from Above

Sitting under, I hear a giggle,
A squirrel jumps, it starts to wiggle.
An acorn falls, a sudden thud,
Who knew nature could be a dud?

Chasing shadows, they play tag,
I laugh so hard, my sides might sag.
Birds drop by and join the fun,
The more, the merrier, oh what a run!

Leaves whisper secrets, they can't keep,
The breeze carries tales, too wild to sleep.
I chuckle hard, my belly shakes,
As the sun sets, the laughter wakes.

Crumbs of joy spread on the ground,
In this cheerful space, bliss is found.
With every chuckle, the world spins right,
Underneath the tree, it feels so bright.

Protective Shade of Time

Underneath, the world feels grand,
In this play-zone, life is unplanned.
A giggling child takes a bold leap,
Into the coolness, a secret keep.

The sun tries hard to peek and play,
But the leaves shout back, 'Not today!'
They dance and sway, a leafy cheer,
While shadows glow and bring good cheer.

Old folks share tales, their voices strong,
In this embrace, we all belong.
A wise old crow caws with delight,
Telling punchlines that take to flight.

In this haven, laughter rings true,
The shade protects, like a giant shoe.
Funny things happen, just take a seat,
Life's silly moments can't be beat.

Nestled Beneath the Leaves

Squished in tight, we hide from rain,
Underneath leaves, we feel no pain.
A puddle forms, splashes arise,
While laughter dances up to the skies.

A ladybug joins our fancy ball,
With tiny shoes, it starts to crawl.
We cheer it on, a tiny champ,
In this wild forest, it's quite the ramp.

Giggling murmurs filter through air,
A cloud of joy, floating with flair.
In secret clubs, our laughter flows,
A symphony only the tree knows.

We count each beat of heart and cheer,
Life in the shade makes troubles unclear.
With friends around, we feel alive,
In this safe nook, we always thrive.

Comfort Found in Stillness

Time slows down, a squirrel is still,
Eyes wide open, with a cheeky thrill.
The stillness hums, creating a tune,
With giggles of grasshoppers under the moon.

A picnic spread, we munch and grin,
With crumbs of laughter, let fun begin.
Nature's comedy, rich and vast,
Moments unfold, they fly by fast.

The breeze whispers, tickling our ears,
Old tree jokes dissolve all our fears.
From bark to branch, the stories flow,
With each chuckle, our spirits grow.

In this peaceful swath, we see the light,
Every funny moment feels just right.
So here we gather, beneath the trees,
In laughter's embrace, we soar with ease.

Delights of the Summer Shade

Under the big, green canopy,
Where squirrels chase happily,
I dropped my ice cream cone,
Now ants have a feast of my own.

Children giggle, dodging drips,
While bees debate on their trips,
A cat naps, donned in sun,
Waking only for a pun.

Laughter dances on the breeze,
As birds chirp, doing as they please,
A hammock swings, holding dreams,
While lemonade flows in streams.

Sunshine laughs, teasing the trees,
Whispers travel with the bees,
In this patch of summer fun,
Who needs the shade? We've all won!

Swaying Dreams of Home

Beneath the leafy fortress wide,
Where imaginations take a ride,
Swings turn into pirate ships,
As giggles spring from playful lips.

A dog's tail wags in the sun,
Chasing shadows, oh what fun!
A lizard skitters, quick as thought,
Stealing heat that summer brought.

Pillow fights with cushions bright,
As sleepy heads drift in sight,
A cardboard box is a racecar now,
Vrooming past, oh look at us go!

In the shade, adventure calls,
With laughter echoing off the walls,
Here in our cocoon of cheer,
Home is wherever we are near.

Crescendo of Nature's Palette

Colors splash from leaf to ground,
Where giggles mix with nature's sound,
A dance of light, a merry sway,
Nature's canvas on display.

Butterflies in funky styles,
Flutter by with silly smiles,
As clouds shape giraffes and cats,
We wave at friendly, flying bats.

Underneath the painted rays,
We concoct our wacky plays,
With shadows forming funny shapes,
Like dancing ducks and prancing apes.

The breeze hums a cheerful tune,
Bouncing high like a bright balloon,
With nature's art, we'll never tire,
In this world of giggles and fire!

Guardians of the Leafy Retreat

In the shade, guardians stand tall,
With silly hats, they greet us all,
A frog dons shades, looking cool,
While a wise owl plays the fool.

Beneath branches, secrets we share,
Spreading laughter everywhere,
A crab sneaks snacks, oh what a thief,
While we munch on endless leaf.

With every rustle, stories unfold,
Of brave ants and treasures untold,
As plump berries roll and race,
It's a berry showdown, we embrace.

Among smiles and nature's charm,
We find a retreat, sweet and warm,
Those funny friends, both furry and wise,
In this leafy haven, life's a surprise!

Beneath the Endless Sky

Beneath a stretch of azure blue,
I laid my plans for mischief too.
The breeze played tricks, and so did I,
With lunch in hand, I aimed to fly.

A squirrel scolded from his throne,
While ants marched in, so overblown.
I tossed my sandwich, made a dash,
But missed my target—a splendid splash!

From in the branches, laughter rang,
As birds performed their goofy slang.
With every bite, I lost my grip,
And joined the dance of nature's trip.

Oh, to be young in this vast expanse,
Where every tumble turns to chance.
The sky, a stage; we're just the clowns,
With fruit-stained smiles and leafy crowns.

Respite in the Green Hues

In cozy green, we found our nook,
A place where squirrels fear to look.
I claimed the sun as my own throne,
While ants rehearsed their busy drone.

There came a breeze, a playful tease,
It swirled my snack into the trees.
The birds wore hats I swear I saw,
I laughed so hard, I dropped my jaw!

With every crunch beneath my feet,
The earth hummed back a joyful beat.
A wiggly worm gave me a grin,
And offered tips on how to win.

In hues of green, the laughter spun,
A cool retreat but never done.
With belly aches from giggles shared,
This is the life, where fun is bared.

Citrus-Scented Memories

A citrus grove beneath the sun,
Where laughter lingers, scented fun.
I played the fool, my cheeks so round,
With lemon juice just pouring down.

A bee buzzed by with mischief's grace,
I ducked and dove to save my face.
But landed smack in orange peels,
A slip, a roll, a world of squeals!

The neighbors peeked from shade nearby,
"Who's that?" they asked with a sly eye.
Yet citrus pranks cannot be missed,
In every bite, a punchy twist.

In slices bright, our heads would spin,
With every snack, more laughs begin.
These memories sweet, they fill the air,
A funny tale beyond compare.

Sun-Kissed Reveries

Out playing games till the daylight fades,
We ride our luck on sunlit blades.
With laughter bubbling in the breeze,
We plotted tricks with perfect ease.

The sun shone down, a golden cheer,
While shadows danced, as if to leer.
We spun and tumbled, brave and proud,
While the grass whispered secrets loud.

In every corner, giggles grow,
With silly faces stealing the show.
A sprig of grass, a crown of green,
Royalty in the field, unseen.

Oh, sun-kissed dreams so wild and free,
Oh, what a sight, just you and me!
With hearts so light and spirits bold,
Our playful tales are worth their gold.

Comfort in a Gentle Breeze

Sitting under a leafy hat,
The world turns silly, oh just like that.
A squirrel playing tricks on a shoe,
While passing pigeons turn blue with the view.

A gust of wind tosses my drink,
It splashes a friend, we both start to blink.
Our laughter dances with leaves in the air,
Guess we'll be sticky, but who doesn't care?

The Umbral Retreat

In shadows deep where giggles hide,
A chair of branches is our pride.
We trade our woes for sunbeam fights,
And crown our heads with fluttering kites.

A bumblebee buzzes with a cheeky show,
As I trip over roots in my toe-to-toe.
Oh, dear friend, don't roll on the ground,
We make quite the scene, laughter abound!

Swaying in the Light

A hammock sways, a soothing dance,
We swing so low, we take a chance.
A breeze says 'hi' with a playful tease,
It tickles my toes, puts me at ease.

Cookie crumbs sprinkle our lounging spree,
A flock of ants begins a decree.
"Who invited the snacks?" they seem to cheer,
Till they realize, 'Oh wait, we are here!'

Tales from the Canopy

The chatter above is pure delight,
As birds exchange secrets, taking flight.
They tell of a worm that danced on a leaf,
We laugh so hard, it's beyond belief.

An acorn drops with a plop and a bang,
A cat leaps high, with a curious twang.
And in this joy, we find a groove,
In this leafy realm, we just can't lose!

Beneath the Silent Watcher

A giant stands with leafy hat,
A throne for squirrels, oh fancy that!
The birds throw parties, sing and chirp,
While ants parade, a tiny burp.

Beneath its boughs, a picnic's laid,
With jammy sandwiches on parade.
Lemonade spills, a sticky pride,
As laughter dances in the slide.

Each gust a tickle, each breeze a joke,
A game of hide-and-seek with smoke.
The sun peeks in through Nature's grin,
While kids run 'round, pure joy within.

In its embrace, we laugh and play,
A belly flop in the sun's warm ray.
With every giggle, we touch the ground,
In this leafy kingdom, joy is found.

Embraced by Nature's Glow

Under the limbs, the world turns bright,
A secret world where dreams take flight.
Dancing shadows play tag with the sun,
While giggles echo, oh what fun!

The breeze whispers tales of old,
While critters convene on stories told.
Nature's jester, in leaves so green,
Makes everyday moments lightly obscene.

With lemonade sips and rubber duck pranks,
Each hiccup of joy ranks among the ranks.
Silly faces in the afternoon light,
Are caught for giggles, oh what a sight!

A canvas of life merges earth and sky,
Chasing butterflies, watching time fly.
Embraced by nature, we take a bow,
In this comedy of life, we live, somehow.

Charms of the Afternoon Light

A wobbly chair, a game of fate,
As sunlight dances, we contemplate.
Each leaf a whisper, a chuckling tease,
Nature's laughter floats on the breeze.

Daisies start gossiping, quite the crowd,
While shadows stretch, feeling proud.
With every giggle, the world feels light,
Under the glow of the afternoon bright.

A cat in the corner, napping free,
Dreams of chasing the dancing bee.
With each little hop, we join the fun,
Creating shadows under the sun.

Every sprinkle of joy is a lovely tune,
As daylight swirls into a balloon.
In this space where smiles take flight,
We catch the charms of the afternoon light.

A Canvas of Nature's Art

Brushstrokes of green, a vivid start,
Nature spills joy, a painter's heart.
Each petal a giggle, each stem a dance,
In the orchard of laughter, we take our chance.

The sky's a canvas, clouds made of cream,
Strawberry ice-cream fuels our dream.
With spritz of water, we're splashed and amused,
As ducks take a waddle, quite bemused.

A treasure chest of whimsical sights,
Curly-haired children chase after delights.
With sand in our toes and grins that just won't part,
We revel together, a canvas of art.

With every tickle from the breeze, we start,
To weave our tales in life's joyous chart.
In this wonderland, with laughter to impart,
We find our way home in Nature's heart.

Heartbeats of Nature

Underneath the leafy crown,
Squirrels dance, they never frown.
With acorns tossed, they play their game,
While the branch shrugs, 'Ain't it the same?'

A bird does laugh, a chirpy cheer,
Sings a tune that all can hear.
Its friends join in, they have a blast,
Oh, what fun! It's quite a feast!

Above them flies a pesky bee,
Buzzing round like it's so free.
But watch it stumble, oh dear me!
Nature's laughs flow like a spree.

As sunlight fades, their joy won't cease,
In this wild world, they find their peace.
From nests to nuts, it's all a game,
Laughter echoes, who can blame?

Dreaming in the Shade

Beneath the giant's leafy arms,
A fox dozes with all its charms.
Dreams of bones and tasty treats,
While ants parade on tiny feet.

A lizard slips with quite a show,
Basking slow, but let's not go!
The shadows giggle, light plays tricks,
Soon the lizard seeks quick fixes.

A butterfly flits, not making plans,
Fumbling softly, it flaps and scans.
In the corners where secrets hide,
It whispers, "Come take me for a ride!"

As sunbeams cast their playful net,
Nature's jesters have no regret.
With joy and laughter, they invade,
In this realm, fun's never delayed!

Beyond the Sturdy Trunk

A shadowy realm of playful glee,
Where critters hop with spontaneity.
Tails wagging madly, voices crass,
Just beyond the sturdy mass.

Chasing dreams in a game of tag,
The tortoise takes a playful brag.
While the hare zooms in with a laugh,
"Catch me quickly, you're half a path!"

The breeze carries tales of jest,
From silly antics to wild quest.
A dance of limbs, and giggles loud,
While nature forms a merry crowd.

As dusk approaches, mischief thrives,
In this sanctuary, fun arrives.
Each creature draws a brand-new plan,
In the heart of life's wild clan!

Lullabies of the Wind

A gentle breeze, a playful tease,
Whispers secrets among the leaves.
It sways the branches, tickles the air,
And cradles the world without a care.

In the dancing grass, a mouse prances,
Trying to catch the wind's quick glances.
It giggles bright, what a surprise,
When the wisp zips right by its eyes!

Clouds drift like sheep on a sunny spree,
Round and round, they're wild and free.
Mocking the sun with a twinkle wink,
Oh, to chase dreams, what do you think?

As twilight sings a lullaby sweet,
The critters settle in for a treat.
With dreams of fun while stars brightly beam,
Nature's laughter is the sweetest theme.

Beneath a Bough of Gold

In the park where giggles play,
A crook-necked bird sings all day.
Juicy fruits and a wobbly squirrel,
Dancing around, such a whirl!

A fellow drops his sandwich down,
A hungry ant wears a tiny crown.
The laughter rolls like summer tide,
As snacks go flying, oh what a ride!

Underneath this leafy throne,
The neighbor's dog claims it as his own.
With a bark and a wag, he hits his mark,
Claiming delicious crumbs, that's his spark!

Children chase a kite that's stuck,
It's tangled high—oh, what bad luck!
But with a sigh, they give it a pull,
The kite's a flyer, and they're the fuel!

Echoes of Forgotten Fragrance

Once a fellow found a shoe,
And wondered whose, oh whose, could it be?
He sniffed and laughed, 'What a strange view!'
'Perhaps it's hiding under a cherry tree!'

A breeze carries whispers of doughnuts past,
Children giggle, wishing it would last.
A squirrel nabs crumbs, the throne he claims,
He's playing king at all the silly games!

'Where do the shadows play at night?'
A cat asks the moon, pondering its flight.
A rustle brings laughter from nearby,
The shadows just giggle and pass by!

The day goes on, full of silly tales,
With sticky hands and mashed fruit trails.
When evening drops, the skies turn bright,
And the echoes dance in the gentle twilight!

Shelter in the Shade

Under leafy arms, a child does sneak,
With ice cream drips, oh what a cheek!
Laughter bubbles, joy on display,
In this cool haven, kids like to play.

A grape-squeezing battle starts to unfold,
With sticky fingers and stories bold.
'The ghost of lunch is coming our way!'
They shout with giggles as they sway.

A chase ignites; someone's on the run,
From an imaginary beast—this is fun!
Parents watch with bemused delight,
While swarms of pests add to the fright!

As the sun dips low, it's time for a tale,
Of forests wild and a pesky snail.
In this cozy nook, laughter prevails,
While memories stick like sweet fruit trails!

Serenade of Leaves

A leaf fell down, a drumbeat's call,
While critters gather, having a ball.
Jumpy frogs join in the parade,
As laughter echoes in the sun's cascade.

One cheeky crow, a bird of delight,
Snatches a snack, then takes to flight.
The crowd erupts in playful cheer,
'Next time, dear bird, bring us some beer!'

A wiggly worm, in fashion's sway,
Shows off his moves in a squirmy ballet.
The wind whispers secrets; they wiggle and sway,
At sunset's cue, they dance and play!

In this leafy nook, joy does abound,
With silly spins, all around.
So here's to the fun beneath sky's dome,
Where laughter grows; it feels like home!

Beneath Verdant Hues

In the shade of green delight,
Chasing birds that take to flight,
Squirrels plotting mischief's score,
Dodging laughter, a playful war.

Group of friends with ice cream splotch,
Sticky fingers, we're a botch,
Slipping on grass, now we tumble,
Under leafy branches, we stumble.

In this cool and leafy nest,
We make jokes that never rest,
Nature's giggles in every breeze,
Life's silly dance is sure to please.

So let's recline on roots that twist,
Make the sun's warmth a friendly tryst,
The grass tickles, oh what a scene,
Under a sky that's bright and keen.

Echoes of Earth's Canopy

The air is thick with silly tunes,
Bouncing around like summer moons,
Here the whispers of trees can tease,
Frogs serenading with utmost ease.

Clouds overhead, in a playful fight,
Chasing the sun, what a funny sight,
Laughter of leaves sways the warm air,
While critters scamper without a care.

Nestled here, with snacks galore,
Ants march in, who could ask for more?
One drops crumbs and starts to flee,
"Oh no," we chuckle, "he's now their tea!"

Beneath the boughs, we plot and scheme,
Daydreams floating like a meme,
In this playful leafy nook,
Life's sweetest joys, we happily took.

Sanctuary of the Warm Breeze

A waft of air, it tickles my nose,
While butterflies dance in their fancy clothes,
A nest of laughter, songs in the breeze,
Here, time is lost with utmost ease.

Warmth on our backs, giggles abound,
As butterflies swirl, it's a silly round,
A dog joins in, just for the fun,
With a wagging tail, he races the sun.

Pillows of grass are our makeshift chairs,
Each dandelion's fluff floats unaware,
And here, we all tell stories absurd,
As nature chuckles, her soft voice heard.

The sun dips low, throwing glittering light,
While shadows dance, they're quite the sight,
With ice cream mustaches and glee untold,
Memories made, more precious than gold.

The Dance of Sun and Shadow

Sunbeams waltz on the ground so bright,
While shadows shimmy, left and right,
Caught in the middle, we squeal and kite,
Directing this show, what pure delight!

Dandelions rise, with hopes so high,
While the crickets chirp, oh my oh my,
A squirrel slides down, cheeky and spry,
In a world made of giggles, we can't deny.

Tic-tac-toe, drawn in the dirt,
All of us playing, no pain, no hurt,
With laughter and joy, we declare our game,
A charming contest, none seek fame.

As daylight fades, we ruckus and play,
In the glow of dusk, we shout hooray,
For in this warm haven where fun's the key,
Life is a dance, we're truly free.

Shadows Playing on Golden Skin

Underneath a leafy dome,
A squirrel slipped, forgot his home.
He tripped and fell on plump green keys,
While giggling loud, he grabbed some leaves.

A cat walked by, all sleek and sly,
Chasing shadows that danced nearby.
He leapt for fun, then took a bow,
But only caught a bug somehow.

With laughter echoes in the air,
Bright rays wiggle everywhere.
A shadow puppet made of twigs,
Turns into knights, then suddenly prigs.

So here we sit, with smiles wide,
In a world of joy, where shadows glide.
With every leap, a cheer we send,
In this sunny realm where giggles blend.

The Edge of Enchantment.

A juggler comes to town today,
With lemons flying, hip-hip-hooray!
He spins around, a twist and shout,
Then slips on juice and takes a clout.

The flies join in, a buzzing band,
They dance around, a groovy stand.
Each wiggle brings a chuckle near,
As juggler smiles, their cheers we hear.

Beneath the dance, the dog does prance,
In search of crumbs, he takes a chance.
But finds, alas, a big, fat bug,
And gives a cough, a funny shrug.

Oh what a sight, this sunny day,
Where laughter bubbles, come what may.
In this enchanted, wobbly space,
We toss our worries, find our grace.

Whispers Beneath the Canopy

A breeze will haunt the leafy round,
Where whispers play and giggles sound.
The ants embark, in single file,
With tiny hats, they strut in style.

A frog commands the leafy choir,
Singing loud, he won't retire.
He croaks a tune about a snack,
Then jumps away with a loud quack!

The sunbirds dart in splashes bright,
Cracking jokes in joyous flight.
While shadows skitter, laughs abound,
In silent games, our hearts are found.

So let us play beneath these leaves,
In chatter's bubble, fun perceives.
With every giggle, spirits soar,
In blissful whispers, we explore.

Sun-Dappled Dreams

Dappled light on grassy ground,
Where daydreams leap and twirl around.
A kid on stilts takes to the air,
While gummy bears fall on his hair.

A picnic spread with pies galore,
But seagulls swoop and call for more.
With every slice, a battle's waged,
As news of crumbs has all engaged.

We laugh aloud at all the sights,
Where ants and kids play funny fights.
The sun dips low, we reminisce,
In dappled dreams, we find our bliss.

So come and join this merry spree,
Where every shadow sings with glee.
With snacks, we weave our tales so bright,
In sun-drenched days, from morn till night.

A Shadowed Respite

In a patch of sun, a cat laid back,
Dreaming of mice and an endless snack,
A lizard joked, 'Hey, pass the cheese!'
While the sun rolled down, they shared the breeze.

A picnic came, with giggles loud,
As kids played tag, beneath the cloud,
One tripped on grass, a tumble and roll,
Shouting, 'I planned this! It's good for the soul!'

Squirrels gossiped on a branch, so spry,
'Who stole my acorn? That sneaky guy!'
They plotted mischief, with twinkling eyes,
While their shadows danced in playful disguise.

As afternoon faded, the fun was grand,
They rode 'the breeze' like a merry band,
In laughter and joy, they found their place,
In nature's arms, there's always grace.

Murmurs of Rustling Foliage

The leaves swayed soft, like dancers on stage,
Whispering secrets from a golden age,
A crow cawed loud, in his worn-out shoes,
'Guess what, folks? I lost my news!'

An ant marched by, with grand parade style,
'I'm the king of snacks, it's been a while!'
He stumbled and fumbled, just trying to eat,
But all his treasures were under his feet!

A breeze played tricks, fluttering high,
Taunting the kites that kissed the sky,
'Watch me swoop!' said a bird with flair,
While the branches chuckled, without a care.

Beneath the laughter of branches all day,
The merry souls found a childlike way,
To bask in joy, where the sun would spray,
In a world so silly, they'd love to stay.

Serenity in the Dappled Glow

Children giggled, chasing after flies,
While shadows danced near, with secretive sighs,
A puppy barked, thinking it a race,
Then tripped on laughter, all over the place.

A grasshopper leaped, with style and flair,
'Catch me if you can!' flew through the air,
While friends gathered round, in dappled light,
Claiming the day as their newfound rite.

One found a hat, old and quite large,
'Is this a crown for my gardening charge?'
They all wore hats, laughing in delight,
Transforming the park into a comical sight.

As the sun began to set, they all agreed,
Nature's a playground, a tapestry freed,
In every giggle, a memory spun,
Where joy and silly antics are never done.

Under the Wing of Nature's Bounty

Beneath the canopy, laughter took flight,
As shadows waltzed, painting the night,
A ticklish breeze played tricks on the toes,
'This isn't a garden, it's where humor grows!'

With crumbs for crumbs, a sandwich was shared,
But ants showed up, and nobody cared,
As giggles erupted from the tallest tree,
'Those ants look like us, sipping on tea!'

Two frogs croaked songs, a rivalry on stage,
Who sang it better, the chubby or sage?
Their croaks echoed bright, like a comical show,
While butterflies floated by, swaying in tow.

As dusk settled in, the joy didn't wane,
Under the stars, they danced in the rain,
For in every moment, life's humor rings true,
A treasure of laughter, for me and for you.

Under the Guardian's Watch

Beneath the leafy giant we sit,
Whispers and giggles, our secret hit.
A squirrel steals lunch, what a cheeky thief,
While we plot to catch him, oh what a relief!

The sunlight dances on our happy faces,
As ants march in single line, to secret places.
We laugh at the shadows, that play on the ground,
In this lively court, joy is always found.

Unspoken Bonds of Green

The branches sway with a silly grin,
As we share secrets, let the games begin.
A chase for a kite that's stuck in the leaves,
We tumble and roll, as our laughter weaves.

The pitter-patter of raindrops may fall,
But we're queens and kings, in our leafy hall.
We dodge puddles like champions, it's pure delight,
In our kingdom of green, everything feels right.

The Hidden Symphony

With a rustle and creak, the branches hum,
The orchestra of insects starts the fun.
A bird hits the high notes, a frog croaks along,
In this whimsical concert, we all sing along.

We dance in the evening, laughter fills the air,
As fireflies flicker, lights everywhere.
A grand finale, when the sun says goodbye,
Leaving behind sparkles in the twinkly sky.

Sunlit Sanctuary of Dreams

We lay on the grass, with heaven above,
Plotting out adventures, we dream of love.
Imaginary dragons, and castles of snow,
In this sunny retreat, our wild spirits glow.

Time doesn't matter, as we drift and play,
In our secret haven, let worries decay.
A picnic of laughter, and stories we share,
Here in our paradise, nothing can compare.

The Stillness Beneath Blossoms

A squirrel placed his order, quite bold,
He asked for some acorns, not too old.
A bird took flight with a chirpy laugh,
Saying, "You won't find them on this path!"

The blossoms giggled as they swayed,
While a bumblebee buzzed, quite delayed.
A cat strolled by, wearing a frown,
"Why's everyone here just messing around?"

A snail claimed the title of the race,
But it took so long, it lost its place.
An ant, with a backpack, hurried to toil,
Said, "I'll catch you all—but first, my oil!"

And there in the stillness, all was bright,
Even the critters danced with delight.
The laughter echoed in the summer air,
While secrets whispered without a care.

Woven in Nature's Embrace

A frog on a log played a tune so sweet,
While crickets and fireflies danced on petite feet.
The wind did a jig, as the flowers grinned,
And leaf after leaf, to the ground, they pinned.

A rabbit popped out, with a top hat in tow,
To announce a grand show with a gleeful glow.
"Who's got the popcorn?" he called with a cheer,
"This theater's the best, come enjoy, my dear!"

A lizard in sunglasses lounged on a stone,
He stretched and proclaimed, "I'm just here alone!"
With each passing breeze, a gossip would spread,
Of petals that whispered of mischief ahead.

As day turned to night in this joyful retreat,
Creatures exchanged tales, all merry and sweet.
In nature's embrace, laughter danced on the breeze,
What a wonderful world, with such simple pleas.

Murmurs of the Evening

As shadows were stretching, the day waved goodbye,
A cricket asked, "Why do the stars seem so shy?"
A hedgehog replied with a shrug of his spine,
"Maybe they're waiting for the moon to align!"

A ladybug laughed, all dressed in her spots,
"I'll race the cool breeze, let's see who's got thoughts!"
A turtle chimed in, quite slow as he went,
"I'll take my time; it's such a nice event!"

The fireflies ignited the dark with their flair,
They joined in a conga, without any care.
The night wore a costume of giggles and sighs,
While owls debated about who'd win the prize.

In this tapestry woven with whispers and cheer,
Nature's own comedy brought all creatures near.
As the evening turned whimsical, laughter rang clear,
A gathering of joy that all would hold dear.

Nature's Quiet Theatre

In the wings of the woods, the curtain did rise,
A raccoon winked at a few fluttering flies.
"Tonight's spotlight's mine," he said with a grin,
"Watch as I juggle these nuts—let the show begin!"

The audience gathered, all eager to see,
A turtle serenaded with not one, but three!
A chorus of frogs sang in jubilant tones,
Echoing laughter that echoed in moans.

A peacock strutted with feathers so grand,
Proclaiming he's king of this whimsical land.
While squirrels did acrobatics, their acts quite absurd,
Cackles erupted; the entire stage stirred.

But the grand finale was a dance of delight,
With all creatures joining in under the light.
Their smiles painted joy, so vivid and bright,
In Nature's theatre, all felt just right.

Gentle Caress of Twilight

In the soft glow, critters hum,
Squirrels dance, oh what fun!
Branches swaying, breezes tease,
Laughter floats among the leaves.

Evening whispers, games begin,
Rabbits hop, and mice chip in.
Underneath the growing dusk,
A glimmer of mischief, a light-hearted brusque.

Fireflies blink like cheeky stars,
Critters play on tiny guitars.
The world a stage, not a care,
As shadows shroud our joyful flair.

With a wink and a playful pout,
Who knew nature had this clout?
In the twilight's gentle embrace,
We find joy, a comical space.

Enchantment Among the Branches

Up high, a bird with a crown,
Chirps a tune, never a frown.
Crickets join in, a quirky choir,
With every note, spirits rise higher.

A squirrel steals a snack or two,
While ants march with a bold crew.
Here in the canopy, life's a jest,
Nature's comedy is at its best.

With laughter woven through the leaves,
Magic twirls, and mischief weaves.
Worms in tuxedos dance with glee,
A hilarious sight for you and me.

In this arboreal fairy tale,
Just watch how each critter sets sail.
Amid branches that sway and shake,
The comedy of life, make no mistake.

Tranquil Embrace of Nature

A sloth hangs low, a wise old sage,
Reading the world from his leafy page.
Witty vines offer clever quips,
While butterflies flaunt their joyful flips.

Hummingbirds zip in a curious race,
With nectar smiles, they quicken their pace.
Beneath the boughs, where giggles grow,
Every creature puts on a show.

Frogs in chorus, croaking away,
Singing ballads of the day.
In this verdant hideaway, life's a song,
In Nature's realm, we all belong.

As shadows stretch, tickling the ground,
Beneath the canopy, laughter's found.
A giggle here, a wink dared,
In this serene chaos, we're all paired.

Paths of Shade and Light

Silly shadows dance on the trail,
Here comes the sun, where mischief prevails.
A floppy hat rolls by with flair,
On this sunny path, who can compare?

Jumping to dodge a gleeful breeze,
As giggles echo through tall trees.
Every nook holds a playful sight,
Like secret jokes in morning light.

A lizard sunbathes, striking a pose,
While bees fashion hats out of rose.
With cheerful hops, we skip and sway,
On these paths where we laugh and play.

Beneath the sky's whims, we wander far,
Finding joy, like a shooting star.
In the embrace of sun and shade,
We share laughter, as memories fade.

In the Veil of Green

Beneath the leafy dome we play,
Where squirrels dance and children sway.
A hidden kingdom of sweet delight,
With giggles echoing, oh what a sight!

The warm sun peeks through emerald layers,
While ants march on like tiny players.
In this jolly court, we're all so free,
But watch out for the sticky honeybee!

Frisbees fly in a lazy loop,
As someone trips, and starts to droop.
Laughter rolls like waves on sand,
With every mishap, the fun is grand!

The boughs above, a shifting maze,
We search for fruit in a holiday haze.
Who knew a picnic could turn so wild?
With juice-stained shirts, we're all beguiled!

A Tapestry of Shadows

In playful shapes, the shadows fall,
A jester's dance, a festival call.
We chase the light and dodge the gloom,
In this great game of nature's room.

A fellow friend climbs high with glee,
He yells, 'Look out! I'm stuck, oh me!'
But as he wiggles, we all burst out,
With fits of laughter and a joyful shout!

Fruits drop down like surprise gifts,
A squishy mess, how the laughter lifts!
Beneath the boughs, we're kings and queens,
In a realm of jokes and silly scenes!

As dusk begins to paint the skies,
The laughter fades, a sweet disguise.
Yet in the night, the tales will grow,
Of playful days and a fun shadow show!

In the Embrace of Silken Shade

Under leaves so broad and wide,
We gather here, our laughter tied.
With snacks and tales, we sit around,
In this cool hideaway, joy is found.

A squirrel scampers, quick and spry,
Stealing crumbs, oh my, oh my!
We throw a nut, it rolls away,
Chasing it, we spend the day.

The breeze whispers secrets, oh so grand,
While ants conspire, a tiny band.
They march in line, so bold and brave,
Yet trip and tumble—what a wave!

With giggles echoing all around,
We feast on sweetness, laughter bound.
In this shady spot, we find our cheer,
Making memories year after year.

Secrets of Summer's Cloak

In a spot where sunlight dips,
We gather with our tasty chips.
The breeze brings whispers, so we cheer,
Hidden secrets that we hear.

A bird drops by for a quick hop,
As we erupt in a silly bop.
We dance around, feet in the air,
With fruity drinks, we have no care.

The insects buzz, a happy song,
But who invited them—right or wrong?
We shoo them off with laughs so loud,
Our merry hearts, they draw a crowd.

With sticky fingers, joy and glee,
We make this summer wild and free.
In this cozy haven, we unwind,
Creating tales that will remind.

The Shelter of Sweetness

In a nook where shadows play,
We sit and munch through the day.
With puddles of juice on our chin,
Yummy laughter, let the fun begin!

A grasshopper hops, what a jolt!
We leap and squeal—big as a bolt.
Bubble drinks and spills galore,
As giggles erupt with every pour.

The fruit on branches swings so low,
A daring challenge—who can grow?
We climb aboard like sailors bold,
Charting adventures, never old.

In our secret world, we are supreme,
With silly schemes, we link our dream.
Wrapped in sweetness, without a care,
We claim this realm—our fruity lair.

Embracing the Orchard's Embrace

Beneath a bough, we gather tight,
In this haven, hearts alight.
With sticky hands and cheery grins,
The fun begins where friendship spins.

A frisbee flies, it's stuck in green,
We try to reach, it feels like a scene!
A leap, a bound, we land with style,
Each flop and tumble makes us smile.

A rumble in the brush nearby,
We turn to see, oh my, oh my!
A raccoon's face, all fuzzy and round,
Stealing snacks from the joyful mound.

So here we'll stay, with laughter bright,
In this little world, our pure delight.
With every sundown, we'll remember the fun,
In this glorious place where we all run.

A Tapestry of Branches

In the garden we play, oh what a sight,
With branches that dance, and leaves in flight.
A swing made of wishes, tied up with a grin,
We laugh as we spin, where fun does begin.

The squirrels throw a party, it's quite the affair,
Dancing and prancing without a care.
They invite us to join with nuts in their paws,
To nibbles and giggles, it's worthy applause!

With a canopy bright, like a quilt on the ground,
We share silly tales, with the trees all around.
The shade is a stage, for our playful retreat,
Comedy gold, can't be beat in this heat!

So let's gather 'round, let the fun never cease,
In this humorous haven, we find our peace.
With nature as our friend, and laughter as reign,
We weave joy like vines, and dance in the rain.

Shadows of Togetherness

Underneath the canopy, laughter fills the air,
Pirates and fairies, hey, what a pair!
Our shadows frolic, like some misfit crew,
Playing silly games, just me and you.

The sun peeks shyly, through leaves of green,
While we tell tall tales, and joke in between.
A cat with a crown swoops in for a chat,
Declares he's the king of this sunny habitat!

In this realm of revelry, time takes a break,
Each giggle a ripple, each twist a remake.
The grass tickles toes, as we tumble and roll,
Creating our moments, they fill up our soul.

So let off the laughter, let joy be our guide,
In the shade, we find solace, where silliness hides.
With friends by our side, and shenanigans grand,
Together we wander, just a laugh and a hand.

Melodies of a Summer's Day

With warmth on our faces, we jump and we sway,
To the tunes of the critters that brighten our day.
A chorus of chuckles, with every sweet note,
Comes from our hearts, as we skip and we float.

The breeze tells a secret, oh listen and hear,
It whispers of joys that we hold so dear.
The ants march in rhythm, like tiny drumbeats,
While we clap our hands to their cheerful feats.

Up high, in the branches, a parrot will sing,
With a voice like a jester, oh what a fling!
We mimic his squawks, add a twist or two,
Creating a symphony, funny and new.

As shadows grow longer, the sun starts to dip,
We share all our giggles in a whimsical trip.
Each note becomes laughter, each note turns to play,
In the garden of joy, we spend our sweet day.

The Whispering Leaves

The leaves start to murmur, with gossips galore,
They plot silly pranks, there's always room for more.
We eavesdrop on secrets, under bright skies,
With nature's accord, we laugh till we cry.

A snail dressed in shades, takes a stroll just so,
Yelling, "Catch me if you can!" oh, how he will go!
His shell is a chariot, we cheer him on loud,
A race for the ages, oh look at him proud!

The moss gives a wink, while the daisies spin round,
Twirling in harmony, off beat and unbound.
A party of flora, where nonsense is rife,
Each moment on repeat, the fun is our life.

So let's sway with the whispers, and dance with the breeze,
As together we bask in this life of pure tease.
With laughter our bond, and cheer in our hearts,
In this lively arena, where joy never departs.

Memories in the Boughs

In the sunlit leaves, laughter soars,
Chasing squirrels as they explore.
A hop, a jump, then a silly fall,
We giggle loudly, hear nature's call.

Ripe fruit drops down, a plop on our head,
Time to dodge, or we'll end up wed.
Beneath the boughs, we craft our dreams,
While ants parade on secret schemes.

We dare each other to climb so high,
To touch the clouds, to kiss the sky.
But slippery branches make us squeal,
As we tumble down, oh what a deal!

With sticky fingers and fruit-stained shirts,
We laugh at our epic, silly alerts.
Each memory, a vibrant hue,
In the shade, where joy feels new.

The Soft Embrace of Solitude

Nestled deep, away from the rush,
A secret spot where moments hush.
Here I sit, with thoughts that dance,
In quietude, I take my chance.

The world feels light as I daydream,
In this lovely, golden beam.
A breeze whispers soft, 'Just be you,'
And I chuckle at the skies so blue.

With nothing but shadows playing games,
And birds that sing their silly names.
Each giggle of sunlight feels so right,
In solitude, I find delight.

I sip on nectar of sweet refrain,
While ants march by in a tiny train.
They seem to laugh and tease me so,
As I revel in this serene show.

Serene Interludes

A little breeze brings tales untold,
Of mischief wrapped in shadows bold.
The laughter here is fresh and bright,
As sunlight dances, pure delight.

Fat bees may buzz, with quite a fumble,
Over flowers, they make their tumble.
I watch their antics, nature's jest,
In laughter, I feel truly blessed.

Kites soar high on playful strings,
While kids below shout out their flings.
Each giggle echoes, wild and free,
In moments draped with harmony.

Life unfolds in hues of cheer,
As fluttering leaves gossip near.
In serene breaths, we find our glee,
Nature's laughter, just for me.

Nature's Quiet Sanctuary

Here amongst the branches wide,
Silly shadows like to hide.
They twist and turn, they prance about,
In this hide-and-seek, I shout.

Leaves rustle with a gentle tease,
As critters scamper, oh what a breeze!
I trip on roots, it's a clumsy dance,
With every step, nature's chance.

Sipping juice from fallen fruit,
I laugh out loud, a fun pursuit.
With every giggle, a tune I hum,
As whispers guide, and sunshine comes.

In this haven, the world stands still,
With nature's joy, we get our fill.
Where simple things bring such pure bliss,
In funny moments, we find our kiss.

Secrets Underneath the Green

Beneath the leaves, the laughter grows,
Where squirrels plot in funny prose.
They steal the fruits, their tiny feet,
While birds complain, they can't compete.

A hide-and-seek with nature's cheer,
The shadows dance, the fun is near.
The ants parade in silly lines,
Marching forth with secret signs.

In the coolness, friends gather round,
Telling tales of silly sound.
Giggling echoes fill the air,
As breezes tangle through their hair.

So many secrets tucked away,
In the green hideout where kids play.
Laughter lingers, life's a game,
Under the leafy, sunlit frame.

Dance of the Dreamers

Under arches made of green,
A whimsy dance, a sight unseen.
The shadows sway in clumsy beats,
With giggling sprouts on wiggly feet.

Bugs join in, with twirls and flaps,
Caterpillars setting up the traps.
The breeze hums tunes of olden days,
While drapes of light perform their plays.

Dreamers spin with carefree joy,
Inventing games, no need for toys.
With every leap, they conjure cheer,
In this frolic, nothing to fear!

Round and round, shadows play catch,
In hues of silly, a perfect match.
The stars would envy such a show,
In the embrace of nature's glow.

Canopy of Comfort

Rest beneath this gentle spread,
A pillow soft, where dreams are fed.
The laughter bubbles like a brook,
In this wild tale, take a look!

Silly shadows play peek-a-boo,
As creatures join, a lively crew.
With every scratch and funny face,
Comes relief in this blissful space.

They sip on sunbeams, sweet and bright,
Creating sparkles, pure delight.
The day drifts by like a balloon,
In the comfort of a leafy tune.

So gather words like seeds, don't spurn,
Let joy unravel, take your turn.
For in this haven, hearts are free,
In the embrace of jubilee.

Reflections of Sunlight

Golden beams dance on the ground,
Bouncing laughter, a joyful sound.
The breezes tickle, shadows tease,
In this light, all worries ease.

With every ripple, the world turns bright,
Chasing giggles till the night.
A parade of colors in the air,
As spirits soar without a care.

Kites in flight, like dreams unbound,
In this warmth, pure joy is found.
As laughter blends with nature's play,
And every moment feels like play.

So let the world become your stage,
Where sunlight flirts with every page.
In the reflection, fun does grow,
Underneath this radiant glow.

The Dance of Sunlight and Shade

Under the sun's playful chase,
Leaves wiggle in a lively race.
Squirrels spin in dizzying turns,
While the grass beneath them burns.

Shadows join in merry jest,
As sunlight winks, they do their best.
Dancing partners, bright and dim,
Twirl on eyesight's edge, so slim.

The ground is a stage, all prepared,
For ants in lines, unbothered, dared.
They waltz along their tiny track,
Scurrying forth, there's no fallback.

In this circus of green delight,
Nature puts on quite the sight.
Giggling blooms like children play,
As laughter echoes through the day.

Sanctuary of Solace

Beneath the branches, laughter rings,
Where birds refuse their normal sings.
They mimic folks with silly flair,
A chorus that's beyond compare.

In this refuge, peace runs free,
While ants bring snacks—a jubilee!
Bees buzz jokes, though none understand,
As flowers giggle, all well-planned.

Sitting still, a wise old snail,
Tells tales of storms and grassy trails.
His voice as slow as molasses sweet,
Drags giggles out—oh, what a treat!

Grinning leaves sway to and fro,
Tickled pink by winds that blow.
Here, in this cozy, leafy nook,
The world outside is but a book.

Stillness Speaks of Time

In the hush where whispers land,
Time wears a big, ridiculous hat.
He stops to chat with squirrels spry,
Who blink and blink, and just sigh.

Ticking is just a game they play,
As shadows join in on the fray.
Watch rubber bands of sunlight snap,
While laughter floats like a power nap.

Moss covers secrets that never age,
In a silent, slow dance on this stage.
A frog croaks jokes in a sleepy dream,
While crickets join in for the theme.

Minutes stumble, tripping on leaves,
While the breeze tickles and weaves.
In this stillness, time's a clown,
With humor stitched in shades of brown.

A World Behind the Leaves

Peeking out from leafy doors,
Are giggles and squeaks, forever more.
Behind each leaf, a secret lies,
Where mischief brews, oh how it flies!

Tiny feet race in and out,
Chasing shadows, without a doubt.
A treasure map of sun and sun,
Where every chase is silly fun.

Among the twigs, a family grins,
Playing tag as daylight thins.
The air is full of playful jive,
As dreams twinkle—what a hive!

Each rustle calls for a joyful jest,
In this world, you'll find the best.
Where mirth and nature intertwine,
In laughter's grip, all beings shine.

Tales of the Greening Realm

In the garden where we play,
Monkey jokes make our day.
Laughter bounces off the leaves,
Tickling spirits, no one grieves.

Squirrels gossip, trees lean near,
Whisper secrets, loud and clear.
A fruit falls with a splat,
And who knew? It's a cat!

Bees buzz round, a sweet parade,
Dancing light in sun's cascade.
Plant your feet, and join the fun,
Underneath the golden sun.

Lizards bask, looking quite chic,
Fashionistas, so to speak.
Nature's jesters, all in green,
What a vibrant scene we've seen!

Comfort in Leafy Company

Underneath the leafy dome,
Squirrels build a cozy home.
Here, the world is full of cheer,
With my friends, I've got no fear.

Caterpillars on parade,
Taking turns in sunshine made.
Chasing shadows, hide-and-seek,
Taking naps, oh so unique!

A robin starts a catchy tune,
We all clap, it's quite a boon.
Just don't ask the ants to dance,
They'll march away, you'll miss the chance!

When raindrops fall, we splash around,
Turning muddy into ground.
With giggles and a hearty laugh,
We float our tiny boats of craft!

A Tapestry of Green and Gold

A tapestry of colors bright,
In golden beams and leafy light.
We weave our stories, bit by bit,
Who knew being silly was such a hit?

Grasshoppers jump for joy in place,
While turtles take things at their pace.
Together they form a funny crew,
Chasing shadows, just like we do!

With every gust, the leaves all dance,
Nature's rhythm, a merry romance.
A butterfly slips on a vine,
"Oh dear!" it shouts, "Not this time!"

Twisted tales of sun and dew,
Crammed with laughter, life anew.
Underneath this vibrant scene,
Every moment feels like a dream!

Odes to Twilight's Refuge

As twilight casts a golden hue,
We gather 'round, just me and you.
The fireflies start their little show,
Lighting laughter that begins to flow.

A raccoon drops by, all dressed in brown,
With mischief painted on its frown.
"Is there room for one more snack?"
"Of course!" we cheer, "There's always a pack!"

The breeze whispers jokes from the past,
Old tales of hijinks we'll forever cast.
Giggles echo through the night,
As shadows dance under starlight.

"Let's build a fort!" an idea takes flight,
With branches and leaves, we're set for the night.
In a world where fun's in every corner,
We live for the laughs, never a mourner!

www.ingramcontent.com/pod-product-compliance
Lightning Source LLC
Chambersburg PA
CBHW070310120526
44590CB00017B/2616